Poetry for the Awakening Soul

Volume I

Is there more to life than this?

Jeanette Tuppen

Pen Press

First published in Great Britain by Pen Press
an Imprint of Indepenpress Publishing Ltd
25 Eastern Place
Brighton
BN2 1GJ

ISBN13: 978-1-906710-43-9

Printed and bound in the UK

A catalogue record of this book is available from
the British Library

Cover design by Jacqueline Abromeit

Dedication

I dedicate this book to
all my Family, the greatest teachers in my life,
especially Ray, Daniel, Lisa
and my gorgeous grandchildren Caitlin, Seth and Rufus.

Thanks

Thanks to my beloved Ray for all the love and support in the many weird and wonderful adventures I have taken upon myself, you were always there to welcome me home.

Thanks to Daniel and Lisa for listening to my poems and also for being the inspiration for many of them.

Thanks to all my family, both near and far, especially my Dad and Mum, brothers Alan and Robert, sisters Jackie and Joanna, all the Allins in America and both Mark and Antonia, new members of the family.

Thanks to all my close friends, especially Marion, Mo, Angela, Judith, Sheila and Roshahnne, who have really encouraged me to get these poems into print. Also other special people, including Nicky, Gillian, Kate, Melanie, Martin and Steve for their wonderful help and support.

Thanks to Marion, Martin, Gillian, Kate, Barry, Mons, Liz, Kathryn, Sally and all the rest of the Friday Meditation Group at Ewell, Surrey, for all their love, support and for being a ready audience for my poetry.

Thanks to Angela, Charlotte, Charis, Judith, Loni, Lucy, Paula and Venetia, members of my own meditation group for all their friendship, love, support and encouragement.

Thanks to Brandon, Kevin and all the Journey team, my life has changed forever, so much love and support to just live in truth.

Thanks to Aeveia and all at Soul Support Systems, the final piece of the puzzle, to live from my heart and soul.

Last but not least, thanks to all my friends and clients who have all been captive audiences for recitals of my poetry.

For the many years I have known Jeanette, I have been inspired by her shining honesty and love. Her remarkable poems are absolutely bursting with it, they are thought provoking and full of self-discovery for us all.

Mo Smith – Reflexologist

These poems will blow your mind, open your heart and soothe your soul… what more could you ask from a book.

Marion Howells
Co founder of Relax for Health – Journey Practitioner

Jeanette's poetry works on many different levels. Her use of and play on words is extraordinary and reveals alternative meanings and new discoveries with every reading. This can lead you into a delicious picnic of revelations and guide you into gentle self-enquiry. Quite simply Jeanette's poetry penetrates the soul and touches the heart.

Kate Farley – Yoga teacher

I love the way that insight has been given into all the poems with some personal experiences and reasons for writing each one – I felt taken on a journey as I read through the book, it's beautiful and powerful and a book I would treasure and keep by my bed – and fall deeper into each time I read it.

Nicky Foster
Journey Practitioner – Pharmacist – Nia blue belt

About the Author

Jeanette Tuppen was born and brought up at 'Rocklands' the family home in East Sussex. It was not until after she married Ray and had her two children, Daniel and Lisa that she started on her healing trail. Her father Max Dickson was an established therapist in both reflexology and massage and was her first teacher, then she followed her own path and has been a healer for nearly 30 years, qualifying in many complementary therapies, including Reflexology, Cranial sacral, Reiki, Lymph Drainage Massage, Deep Tissue Massage, NLP, Voice Dialogue and the list goes on and on. She has also taken a four-year Shamanic training course.

Then after her mother Nancy died, she had a complete breakdown. This is when she found 'The Journey' and this process literally changed her mind and changed her life, from barely coping to being fully alive, well most of the time!

From this she learnt to look within for her answers and to trust in herself. Then the poems came along, originally as a journal of her own emotional and spiritual awakening; however when she shared these poems with her family and friends, they were also inspired and moved by them. So after many requests for copies, the book was born, in the trust that it will benefit all those searching souls to discover their true selves by just being who they already are.

Also in reading and sharing the poems, she has come to know herself better and liked what she found, most of the time, and even when she didn't she learned to open her heart to meet all that was present and in doing so found peace and wholeness, a joy of life she had never known before.

Poetry Contents List

Foreword

Jeanette Tuppen is a poet, shaman, artist and intuitive healer so there is more to this than just the poetry. Jeanette takes you on a journey of exploration following the events in her life. She dives deeply into her own emotions to discover wholeness, peace, truth and love.

The poems are inspired by the words found within words. How amazing to realise that both 'silent' and 'listen' have the same letters as do 'earth' and 'heart' and that 'lost' is in 'stolen' and 'give' is in 'receiving'.

This poetry is uplifting and inspirational, whilst also deep and thought provoking. It has a rawness and freshness in its simplicity, in both the questions asked and the answers given, as revealed in the poem 'Beliefs'.

Beliefs

Of course *life is* an illusion,
Why else would live and *life*,
Both have *lie* in them.

And as for your *beliefs,*
Why would you trust any of these?
For here there's found both *lies* and *fibs.*
And *I* know they say, ignorance *is bliss,*
But do you really want to spend,
The rest of your *life,* feeling like this.

So what *is* the truth that *lies* beneath?
The *self* to *see* in your *beliefs,*
To *feel, if I* be, then *life* just *is.*
Be life or *belief*
Your choice.

Poetry for the Awakening Soul
Volume I
Is there more to life than this?

I write poems
of
Words within words.
It may seem absurd
to write
Poems of words within words,
But the things that they say
Just blow me away.

I never thought of myself as a writer, let alone a poet, until several important life events came together and I was moved to put pen to paper.

The first was the death of my mother, which led to a breakdown. In my recovery I found that so much of me had been buried alive and I was shocked to discover how numbed out to life I was.

Then three books crossed my path and helped bring out my creative talents, and in the process helped healed my soul.

The first was *The Journey* by Brandon Bays.

The second was *A Course in Miracles* scribed by Helen Schuman, Ph.D.

And the third was *The Artist's Way* by Julia Cameron.

All three of these books helped me to discover and then recover myself and my creativity and I am so grateful – thank you.

This book is my journey to wholeness and the poems are arranged in the order I wrote them. Each word came to me in perfect timing when I was ready and willing to meet whatever appeared in the poetry. Some of the poems have taken years to write. They required me to face parts of myself I was not able to go to at that time, only to present themselves again at a later date. As I have become more willing to accept myself (especially my rage) and been able to open my heart even when completely overwhelmed, I have found peace.

My first attempt was while following the Artist's Way, a 12-week course with weekly tasks, one of those being to write a prayer.

A Journey Prayer

I would see you as my friend
Remembering all is part of me
And so reveal myself.
Then as this journey unfolds
Within I find my way
To source.
All of creation right here in my heart
Once open and flowing
Fills me with love.
Wanting to share this greatest of gifts
With all those around me,
Diving ever deeper
Into this bubbling cauldron of loving creation
Ready to serve the feast of the day
Whatever that is, let it shine forth
Honouring this divine, creative source.
Thank you God for all these gifts
For in welcoming my own creation
I put my hand in yours
And let Grace lead the way.
Thank you, Thank me, Thank all.

* * *

The next major event was another death, this time my father-in-law. I loved this man as much as my own dad and in his passing I wanted to honour what a glorious soul he was, and it was poetry that helped me express this perfectly. So here is my second attempt.

Ode to Len

The cheery wave, with hand held high,
The smiling face, the twinkling eye,
The welcome greeting to all who pass,
The bone crushing grip from hands that grasp,
Ah yes, those hands, such powerful hands,
That should you happen to greet,
With a pat on the back,
You're sent flying off your feet.
A powerful man, a peaceful man,
Leonard Thomas Tuppen.

In the garden, most every day,
Rain or shine, come what may,
Never rushing, steady going,
Planting, digging, weeding, sowing,
Cheerfully whistling, happily working,
Readily stopping, joyfully greeting,
Gladly passing time of day,
With all, who come along his way.
A happy man,
A hard working man,
Leonard Thomas Tuppen.

Now if there's something, you wanted to know,
Of planting a garden, or what to grow,
Len was the man, you needed to ask,
Nothing too little, or great the task,
And if a molehill or two, should appear,
Just mention his name, to fill them with fear,
They'd pack their bags, and off they would go,
Never again, their faces to show.
A wonderful man,
A wise, wise man,
Leonard Thomas Tuppen.

This man was known, as the tomato king,
He'd talk to his plants, and he would sing,
If Prince Charles can do it, so can I,
And they'd grow so tall, they'd reach the sky,
Enough tomatoes, I would have to mention,
For you, me, the village,
And still feed a small nation.
A gardening man,
A generous man,
Leonard Thomas Tuppen.

Now for something, that's a favourite of mine,
Having sampled my share, of Len's home-made wine,
From garden and hedgerow, kitchen and store,
Gathering ingredients, from whatever he saw,
And once you have tasted,
Knowing quickly the truth,
Most of it, quite delicious,
All of it, 90% proof.
A joyful man,
A jolly man,
Leonard Thomas Tuppen.

There are some of you, who knew him well,
With many stories, you can tell,
From a time gone by, quite long ago,
Of football skills, that he could show,
Each Saturday morn, with his clean kit on,
Out to the field, he would run,
Charging this way and that, as fast as he could,
Displaying the talents, of his cultured left foot.
A sporting man,
A special man,
Leonard Thomas Tuppen.

Out and about, the village he'd go,
A ten-minute walk, that's all you know,
But two hours later, back home he would show,
For stopping to greet all, is what made him slow,
He liked to talk, he loved a joke,
Of football and cricket, he often spoke,
Happy to greet all, as friends don't you see,
For Barcombe was where, he most liked to be,
And you are all part, of his great family.
A friendly funny family man,
A caring, cuddly, kindly man,
Leonard Thomas Tuppen.

Now some of us, are luckier than most,
Family and friends, those who were close,
Whenever a greeting, he'd be so glad,
Or if he saw you, weary or sad,
His big arms around you, and he would squeeze,
A force so powerful, you'd hardly breathe,
The warmth surrounding, so full of love,
For Len could always, give a great hug.
A big hearted man,
A bear hugging man,
Leonard Thomas Tuppen.

A father, grandfather, brother and friend,
My heart full of love, I willingly send,
To this wonderful man, that we all know,
So hard to leave, and let him go,
A memory though, that all can keep,
For Len would say laugh, to those that weep,
So just remember the sun, as his shining face,
The singing birds, his whistling grace,
The gentle breeze, his warm embrace,
And know that you are never, so very far apart,
When you keep this bright light shining, deep in your
        heart.
A loving man,
A laughing man,
Leonard Thomas Tuppen.

And all the things, I've spoke today,
Just point a finger, to his way,
For he was so much more than this,
More than I can ever say,
It is only in your heart of hearts,
In that special place,
That you may ever truly meet,
And know his warm embrace,
A gentle man,
A glorious man,
Leonard Thomas Tuppen.

* * *

The next poem came along after a visit to my friend Steve, an amazing homeopath and married to one of my very best friends Mo.

Well, as usual, in my sessions, all this grief and sadness came up and Steve questioned what I needed to believe in, for all of this to be true, then he pointed out that there was a **lie** in the middle of be**lie**ve. Well this stopped me in my tracks because it was true, there it was, this lie in the middle of be**lie**ve and this triggered off a new poem. Thank you, Steve and Mo.

Believing

While pondering awhile on believing,
I noticed a lie in the middle,
New information I'm now receiving,
To help me solve this riddle,
All this time I've been believing,
My experience of life all I knew.
For so long I have been deceiving,.
Because nothing's so far from the true.

So what if believing, is only what I be living,
There's a question I'd ask that is new,
What kind of God must I believe in?
For all of this to be true.
On the one hand I've been living,
A life of struggle, limitation, not enough,
And yet, deep down, on the other, I'm perceiving.
A God, in abundance, all embracing, full of love.

So the answer to this I'm now giving,
A solution I've found for myself,
Is to take this life you've been living,
And welcome all that's present and felt.
Then bringing your two hands together now,
Staying open and very curious,
Wondering what this is really about, and asking how?
Do I bring love to all of this?

* * *

The poem 'Believing' really got me thinking about life, and I started to wonder why my life felt like such a struggle, because in theory I had everything I could possibly want to be happy, a loving husband, two beautiful children, work that I loved, living in the house of my dreams... and yet there was something missing, I still did not feel truly happy. Then I realised, for as long as I could remember I have been searching for something, something that if only I could get right, would stop the search. The problem was so much of me felt wrong.

Wrong

The moment I'm made wrong,
It causes so much pain,
I immediately close down,
Not to feel again …   Then I stop listening.

And I hate how I feel,
Whenever I'm made wrong,
Not okay or good enough,
And I don't belong…   Then I stop listening.

Words may then be spoken,
All fly above my head,
As a rage burns deep within,
All other feelings dead…   By then I've stopped listening.

And now I'm wondering…

What is it that's wrong?
These feelings in me now,
If only I could own,
Be present and ask how…   Then maybe I'd start listening.

So, instead of closing down,
The truth I want to know
When I own now, I've won
Then I go on and grow...   Now I'm listening.

Own, now, won,
Go on grow,
Are all words found,
In the letters of WRONG... How cool is that.

* * *

Now I was interested in listening, what did it mean to listen? How did I do it, this listening thing? I suppose I needed to stay open, to stop what I was doing and to pay attention. Then imagine my surprise when I noticed that both **listen** and **silent** had exactly the same letters in them, and then you could have blown me over with a feather when I realised that **stillness** also used these same letters. This now set the trend, of seeing poems in the words within words.

All the words in italics are found within the title poem, I do give myself poetic licence to use each letter as many times as I want!

Listen

In silent,
I listen,

In stillness,
I listen,

Still,
In silent,
I listen.

* * *

I found myself looking differently at words to see all they held within them, it became quite an obsession and made it very difficult to read anything! As I relaxed more and really started to listen I noticed certain words would leap from the page and I started to make a note of them. These words I used to write the poems with, always seemed relevant to whatever was going on in my life at that moment.

I was looking at my life differently now and was wondering why I did not think I deserved to be happy, then it hit me, I did not feel I was worthy.

Worthy

Why worthy?
Who worthy?
Try worthy?
How worthy?
Why worry?

* * *

I was questioning more and more, what was life really about anyway? Then I noticed that **evil** and **devil** were just **live** and **lived** spelt backwards. This got me thinking, what if evil is just the reflection of live, not the real thing but a belief we have about life, then along came the next poem.

Live

Born to be free experience and *live*,
When made to feel wrong, down comes the *veil*.
Filled with anger and rage, feelings so *vile*,
Uncontrollable urges, now believed *evil*.

Then facing the demons once thought *evil*,
Diving deeply into those feelings so *vile*,
Resolving old issues and lifting the *veil*,
Now freeing the soul to be fully a*live*.

* * *

I became very occupied writing my verse, it was so much fun, words were just leaping out at me, begging me to write a poem about them. I noticed that **passion** could simply be **'pass I on',** yet another poem in the making and then I saw that '**I am'** is in **champion** and **me** was in **home.**

Words to Remember

Some words to remember
Wherever you may roam
I am is in ch*am*pion
And *me* is in ho*me*.

* * *

I also started to look at words that sounded the same, but were spelt differently, like hole and whole. These two really got me going because they feel like both ends of the scale. Whereas a hole is nothingness, empty by its nature and whole is the complete thing, fullness by its nature. Then there was holy – well, where did that fit in.

Hole, Whole, Holy

A hole gets larger,
The more that's taken,
It's the emptiness left,
Clear and open.

The whole, all there is,
Everything included,
Nothing left out, forgotten,
Or excluded.

Holy is the divine,
The nothingness from,
Which all things,
Are born.

So from the hole,
The whole,
Is created,
Holy.

* * *

I had also been noticing how differently people view their worlds. How some saw their cup half full, while others saw their cup half empty. So one focused on fullness and the other focused on emptiness, this got me thinking about how our language shaped our world.

So what if instead of seeing problems and difficulties, each situation was now seen as a challenge? How much would life transform? Then when I saw '**angel calls'** was in **challenges,** well this just blew me away yet again.

Challenges

Challenges, *a chance* to *heal*,
For everyone, *each* and *all*,
To *change* the viewing *angles*,
And hear the *angel's call*.

The *challenger's* task, to free the *rage*,
To *search* within and find what's *real*,
A chance to free the inner *sage*.
And *hear* the *angel's call* to *heal*.

So now when feeling *challenged*,
In search of where to *land*,
Just remember it is *an angel call*,
Come to give you *a hand*.

* * *

So what happens to this life when instead of seeing problems and difficulties, each situation is now met as a challenge, maybe no longer seen as an enemy but as a friend or ally. I know there is a saying, 'What does not kill you makes you stronger.' What if this is really true and these challenges are here to help us grow, to find our own inner strengths and are truly our friends, if we let them be. Then I noticed **fiend** was held in **friend** and a new poem was born.

Friend

Fiend or *friend,*
Find or *end.*
Nerd or *red,*
Fired or *fed.*
Rend or *dine,*
Fend or *fine.*
Ride or *dire,*
Fried or *fire.*
Fin, fen or *fie,*
Din, den or ... *die.*

* * *

I found that writing these poems was not only deep and meaningful (and I can do that very well) it was also great fun, I was really enjoying myself with all these new talents. As I said at the beginning I have never thought of myself as a writer, let's face it I managed to fail my English GCE O level three times, the first time with a grade 9, which basically means I spelt my name right, so this was bringing me great joy, I felt ecstatic and then saw in the word **ecstasy,** '**say yes',** and I felt this so fitted, when we say yes to life, maybe life says yes back to us.

Ecstasy

Ecstasy
Act easy
Say yes
Tease.
Yes stay
At ease
Eat tasty
Ecstasy.

* * *

I am not sure how to introduce these next poems, other than to just dive right in, so here goes. I have always believed in a higher deity and because I was brought up Christian I have called this being God. I have however questioned the lack of the feminine within this religion, especially with God the Father, Son and Holy Ghost, I thought at least this Holy Ghost or Holy Spirit might be feminine, but apparently not! So my question has been where in nature does creation take place with just three male entities and no sign of a woman.

I have now found a divine feminine that I am free to love and honour, her name is Grace!

God and Goddess

God,
Go and *do.*
Goddess
Goes and *does.*

* * *

Have you noticed that most masculine words are found within the feminine words, that is all except masculine and feminine of course, well I have and this is what I found, **God** in **God**dess, **male** in fe**male**, **man** in wo**man** and **he** in s**he.** And yes you are right maybe I do need to get out more! So this is the next part of **Goddess and God.**

Goddess and God

Within Goddess there is God,
Within female there is male,
Within woman there is man,
Within she there is he.

So the feminine is inclusive,
Yielding, holding and open,
And the masculine is exclusive,
Focused, powerful and strong.

These are just energies,
We all hold within,
And to make us complete,
We need both of them.

Without God, man, male and he,
Woman would be dess-wo-fe-s.
Without Goddess, woman, female or she,
Man would be… lost.

Just in case you are wondering, **dess-wo-fe-s** are the letters left over after the masculine part of the word has been removed.

* * *

Still searching for answers and not knowing where to look I came across the word '**nowhere**' and suddenly realised that the answer was right there staring me in the face, '**now here**'.

Nowhere

Nowhere
now here
her, here and now
he, where and how.
Who won
no one
we're on
our own.

When and where
now and here
when and how
here and now
we won
when we
own now
we're one.

* * *

Then I noticed that so many of the words I used, had the letters E A R in them and I was reminded that we have two ears and only one mouth so that maybe we need to listen twice as much as we need to speak.

Ear

Maybe anger, rage and fear
All have a common intent
With ear, are and era
Listen, to your beingness, in this moment.

So instead of making wrong
Please listen to their intent
When you own now you've won
For the gift of now is the present.

And if ever feeling scared
How about reading it as sacred
Also listen to words with ear
In silent and see where it may lead.

Yes now is the time to listen
And a really good place to start
Is to open up to the Earth
And listen with your heart.

* * *

I have often wondered what enlightenment is, there is a saying, 'Those that know, don't know, and those that don't know, know'. So what is it all really about, maybe a solving of riddles, who knows?

Enlightenment

So what is *enlightenment*?
There's *lie, tie* and *nigh in enlightenment,*
There's *light, tight, night* and *might,*
And *lint, tint, hint* and *mint,*
There's *let, met, get* and *net,*
And *lit, hit, git* and *nit.*

There's *eight*, *nine* and *ten* in *enlightenment,*
There's *he*, *him*, *gent* and *men,*
And *me, mine, thine* and *them,*
There's *Len, Tim, Nigel* and *Neil,*
And *Genie, Meg, Hettie* and *Mel.*

There's *hinge, minge* and *tinge* in *enlightenment,*
There's *letting, netting, melting* and *thing,*
And *length, tenth, item* and *theme,*
There's *lighten, tighten, element* and *elm,*
And *title, entitle, tenement* and *helm.*

There's *glee, glint* and *gem* in *enlightenment.*
There's *teen, gene, tin* and *gin,*
And *tile, mile, Nile* and *nil,*
There's *tilt, hilt, gilt* and *melt,*
And *teeth, teem, meet* and *mitt.*

There's *gentlemen, genet* and *gel* in *enlightenment,*
There's *nee, neigh, leg* and *lei,*
And *mingle, tingle, tehee* and *melee,*
There's *gentle, gentile, gen* and *gilet,*
And *lenient, linen, liege* and *legit.*

There's *time, line* and *then* in *enlightenment,*
There's *mite, eel, tit* and *hen,*
And *lithe, tithe, inlet* and *thin,*
There's *nettle, mettle, linnet* and *tenet,*
And *intent, entente, gimlet* and *I'm in it,*
So what is *enlightenment?*
I don't know!

Those of you, who know
About *enlightenment*
May know
That I know about *enlightenment.*
Those of you, who don't know
About *enlightenment*
May think, I don't know too
Either will do,
It's really up to you!

* * *

Yes I know it is another riddle. Well if you can't beat them, join them.

There are so many things that puzzle me and after investigating enlightenment and getting nowhere fast, I decided to turn my attention to love, wondering if here is where I could find what I was looking for, as it is said 'Whatever the question the answer is love.' So this was my next quest, to seek out words with 'LOVE' in them.

Love

As source de*velo*ps within me,
I am resting in deep love,
As source en*velo*pes, setting free,
I am resting in open love,
As love opens all closed doors.

As source s*olve*s all problems rising,
I am resting in love so much,
As source res*olve*s all conflicts fighting,
I am resting as lovers re-love,
Now embracing all once more.

As source *evol*ves, the way now leading,
I am resting in love's love.
And in the reflection of *evol*ution,
No it u *love*.
Yes, know it you *love*!

* * *

Still on the theme of love, I noticed that both **violence** and **violate** had the words **live** and **love** in them and I was wondering how that fitted in the scheme of things. Then when I saw **voice** was also in **violence**, a picture began to emerge, that is a picture of words.

Violence

There's an unknown *voice in violence,*
That's desperate to be heard,
To *live in vile* and *evil* ways,
Its only way to serve.

There's a *lone lie in violence*,
That's far from being *nice*,
And because you believe it fully,
It grips you like a *vice*.

There's *live* and *love in violence*,
It's hard, I know that's true,
If only you could hear this *voice*,
But it's really up to you.

For *no one* can *convince*,
Against a being's will,
No matter how loud that *voice*,
You'll be *unconvince*d still.

But *once* you hear that call,
Know it is your choice,
To see the *lie,* and lift the *veil*,
And find *love*'s own clear *voice*.

* * *

26

My next poem came to me as I wondered about unconditional love. What is it, and what does it really mean? I had heard it spoken about and yet never seen it practised, there still always felt like there were things that needed to be changed or got rid of. Then I noticed that **grace** was in **gr**ievan**ce**s and it came to me that if we were able to face our grievances then maybe these would be the key to unlock the door of unconditional love, where everything was accepted and loved, with no conditions.

Grievances

Release the *grace* in grievances,
And *see* how they *can serve*,
They're all here for a reason,
And it's their time to be heard.

Listen to their mournful cry,
And *give* them time to *grieve*,
Once welcome these emotions *rise*,
And flow, like water through a *sieve*.

Anger and *rage are* held *in* them,
Their truth, not *ever seen*,
Never to *see* the light of day,
Since it's you that holds the *rein*.

But what if you could change the *scene*,
And face the *river* of your fears,
Even when it makes you *cringe*,
Be the someone, who really *cares*.

So give them chance to *reign* a while,
Yes give them chance to *sing*,
See what it *is,* they have to say,
Then *receiving,* what they bring.

And do you know the difference,
Between *grievance* and *receiving*?
There's *an 'a' in grievance*,
And *an* extra '*i*' *in receiving*.

'A' is something outside yourself,
And not a part of you.
Where *as* 'I' is your very self,
And the part that you *see* through.

* * *

Still on the search for acceptability, I noticed several words with 'soul' in them, how amazing to see that 'solution', transforms into 'soul on it', so short and sweet here is my next offering.

Soul

Soul is in y*our*se*l*f,
It's also in il*lus*io*n*,
And know your *soul* is on it,
In every *solu*tion.

* * *

So are you willing to embrace all of who you are, even the shadow side? And what if this part of us, is only in the dark because we are unwilling to go there, to bring it into the light, to embrace all of our beingness?

Embrace

Within *embrace*,
I *am me,*
Full of *care*,
And free to *be*.

Within *embraces*,
I *am me,*
When it *scares*,
I *am* the one,
Who really *cares*.

Within *embraced,*
I am me,
Made to *be*,
To *bare* my soul,
And *dare* to *dream*,
I *am* the *cream*.

Within *embracing*,
I am being,
Anger and *rage*,
Caring and *racing*,
Yes it's *me*,
All *embracing*.

* * *

The next two poems are about the need to protect, to save ourselves and others from entering this dark world of unwanted feelings, to stop the pain – anything rather than go there. How we try to rescue in order to take away that pain. Well, I will tell you now it does not work, never has and never will, all that happens is now, the ante has to be upped.

Rescue

To the *rescue*,
Curse or *cure*,
Use or *user*,
Right on *cue*,
Which one are you,
Are you *sure*,
Or do you *rescue*,
To be *secure*

* * *

I have noticed that when we get upset there is often someone around to comfort us, to make it better but what if in the comforting we are made to feel it is not okay to feel the emotions that are present, just a thought.

Distress

Please don't *distress* yourself,
Hold it all in like everyone else,
To see you in so much pain,
Reminds me of my own again,
So there, there, there,
Take comfort from me,
Now I won't have to look and see,
This pain is far too much to bear,
Do what you have to,
I don't care.
Just please don't *de-stress* yourself,
Hold it all in,
For everyone else.

* * *

After all this deep and meaningful stuff I saw the word 'bounty' and this wonderful word filled me with pleasure, to think that all of me could be embraced, made welcome and that indeed held the answer to all my longings, well what joy.

Bounty

You too
Are found in
Bounty
And
I wonder if
It is
The same bun in *bounty*
That is found
In
Abundance.
I think it is
And
I want some,
To bite this *bun*
Is so much fun
Yum, yum, yum,
Thank you *bun*.

P.S. This bun is also found,
In the leaping bound,
And
Bouncy, bouncy, bouncy.

* * *

Now for something completely different, I had been wondering about the ego and after some investigation; discussions, seminars and the reading of many books, I came to the conclusion that the ego was much maligned and in fact seemed to be the new devil, to be got rid of ASAP. Well ever rebellious and still wondering about this unconditional love, which to me meant that everything was acceptable – I mean unconditional means no conditions, doesn't it. Also I noticed that the letters EGO were found in **GO**DD**E**SS, so here was my next poem.

Ego

Ego is the greatest gift,
The *Goddess* gives to you,
Without it this amazing self,
You would never view,
For in your very beingness,
Nothing's ever new,
Always knowing who you are,
And everything that's true.

Ego takes you by the hand,
So you can forget,
Still a memory of who you are,
Only now you're separate,
And this is the gift,
The pleasure that you get,
The exquisite joy of oneness,
Each time you reconnect.

Ego does the best it can,
Bless its little heart,
Always seeking the way home,
No matter where you start,
And the armour for protection,
The wall that keeps apart,
Still holding all the clues,
To remind you of your path.

Ego is like quick silver,
A slippery, slithering eel,
And each enlightened moment,
Tries so desperately hard to steal,
To capture something missing,
An emptiness, there's longing to fill,
Believing *E*verything *G*ood is *O*utside,
And nothing in here is real.

So *ego* tells these stories,
And the truth is, they're all lies,
They create a unique reflection,
To bring a mirror before your eyes,
And maybe you are wondering,
How to see through this disguise,
Well, it's only in this moment,
That truth, is ever realised.

Ego is just *ego*,
A game of hide, and go seek.
The awareness of awareness,
When you are awake.
It's just the story teller,
NOT
The devil incarnate,
Only *ego* wants to rid itself, of *ego*,
When nothing's here, to celebrate.

Yes *ego* is the greatest gift,
The *Go*ddess gives, it's true,
To experience this amazing self,
So many times a new,
Each time we take this journey,
For this special view,
Joy of joys, love and laughter,
On coming home… to you.

* * *

Even with all this awareness, I noticed I still could become very angry with things that did not fit into my world and how I thought life should be, (I know very arrogant of me). I own up, I realise how intolerant I am to so many things, and in that moment of intolerance I am closed, my heart is closed, to all the many possibilities available. So with tolerance there is an opening, and my world expands.

Tolerance

Tolerance is *a talent*,
Here *to* help you *learn*,
To clean up your *act*,
Then trust you will *earn*,
To create clear pathways,
So you're *not alone*.

Tolerance and understanding,
Take you out of *trance*,
Once alert, you *can care*,
React and enhance,
To create clear pathways,
And give peace a chance.

Tolerance brings compassion,
To another's point of view,
To listen without bias,
Will give you a clue,
To create clear pathways,
To those different from you.

* * *

This next poem was written by Lucy West a member of my group, and it had a huge impact on my writing, helping me to step out of the box with my poems. Thank you, Lucy.

Self Doubt

Within *self doubt* there's *lots of foul foes,*
There's *debt* and *dole*, and *slut* and *slob*,
There's times before where you have *bled*,
And times ahead for you *to sob*,
There's all the times that you've been *told*,
And there's every moment you're getting *too old*,
There's all the wrong paths down which you were *led*,
And all the times you hid in your *bed*,
There's every time you've been a right *sod*,
No wonder you're left in the end on your *tod*.
There's all the *lust* you shouldn't have had,
There's all the bad things that you *bet* would happen,
And a whole lot more that you just *let* happen.
There's all the times you're not feeling *bold*,
And don't *feel* the power *to let* your *best* un-*fold*.
And every time you're just breaking through,
You realise you're actually,
Totally and utterly,
Completely, unstoppably
L O S T !
But:
Whenever you're *lost* in the winds *of self doubt*,
Somewhere within there's a *bud*,
If you just allow all the *blood to be bled,*
All the *sobs to be* said.
If you just allow yourself *to be told,*
Allow yourself *to* grow real *old*,
Go down the paths, down which you were *led*,
Enjoy the times you hid in your *bed*,
Love yourself for being a *sod*,
Know it's ok *to be* on your *tod*.

37

Feel the *lust* that everyone has,
And know the *dust* that's made you *feel* a waz!
Laugh at things you *bet* would happen,
And laugh even more at the ones you *let* happen!
Allow yourself to not *feel bold*,
And know the best will un-*fold*.
For within your *self doubt*,
Even your *self doubt*,
In all of you,
Is
Your
S O U L.

* * *

Following on from 'Tolerance' and 'Self doubt' I became aware that I had to make loads of judgements in order to justify my behaviour and reactions. I also realised that nothing was safe from my judgements and that the person I judged the most was myself.

Judgements

It's *just me* on the *menu*, when I sit with all my *judgements*,
My *guts* tied up in knots, at the bottom of this pit that I've *dug*,
Stuck in all this *gum*, feeling such a *mug*,
A huge *dent* in my soul, not knowing how to *mend*,
With a *gun* against my head, if only this would *end*,
As the enemy within brings me closer to the *edge,*
My identity a *smudge*, please no not another *nudge*,
Oh how I wish I did not have to *judge*.
Hang on a minute, what is this I *see*,
Right in the middle, a *gem*, and it's waiting there for me.

If you *must judge me*, know I'm the one, who *just gets* your
    needs met,
And you're the *mug* if you think these rules are in stone firmly
    set,
So is this the *gem*, stuck in all this *gum*,
Beneath a load of *dust* and a great big pile of *dung*,
Must I strip it *nude* and change the *tune* I've *sung*,
It *seems* a lot of work, in *mud* and *guts* and *suet*,
I *guess* it *must* be worth it to sing a different *duet*,
For when I *see* the whole of *me*, instead of *just* a *segment*,
I can *see* it's worth it all, to find this golden *nugget*.

* * *

You may be realising that I am prone to taking myself way too seriously and you are right, I need and want to lighten up, and I have found laughter to be a great way to achieve this. Yes, laughter truly is the best medicine.

Laughter

Let there be *laughter*,
*Huge, great rag*ing *laughter*,
Let the earth be *true* to *laughter*,
And surrender to *the rule* of *laughter*.
Let hate and *rage, argue* and *glare* in *laughter*,
It's never too *late*, to open *the gate* and *alter all* in *laughter*.
Let your *heart rate* rise, in *the heat* of *laughter*,
Once out of *the rut, let* your *gut,* be *real* in *laughter*.
Let all hurt heal in *the heart* of *laughter*,
And *gather* as one, in *the glue* of *laughter*.
Let her rattle Hera and *hag,* to *eat* up *laughter*,
And *he treat Earl* and *thug* to *the art* of *laughter*.
Let Hera, hag, Earl and *thug, tell the tale* of *laughter*,
And *urge all* to remove *the halter* and be *at large* in *laughter*.
Let your *heart hug the earth* with *laughter*,
And *hear the tear, that'*s *true* in *laughter*.
Let age alert you to *the lure* of *laughter*,
And be *a rag-tag*, to *the tug* of *laughter*.
Let your *ear* now *hear the* call*, to *tell all* in *laughter*,
Heart felt, *earth* filled, *heal*ing *laughter*.

* * *

My family has always meant a lot to me and looking for approval from them has been top of my list for a long, long time and yet now I realise this family of mine has been my greatest teacher in self-acceptance. Also I have found that through life's journey, my family has expanded to include many wonderful soul sisters and brothers that fill my life with joy.

Families

Fame and *lies* and *miles* of *smiles*
The *flame* that *flies* the *same* for *miles*
Male or *female*
Whatever your *aim*
There's *life* to *fill*
And doors to *slam*
And *if* you *fail*
Or ever *fall ill*
There's *a* place that's *safe*
And *a* ready *meal.*
Through *lame* and *slime*
When you *feel small*
And *life's a leaf*
That's about to *fall,*
Just *smell* the place,
Where all this *lies,*
And *see,*
All is,
I am me,
In *families.*

P.S. You may realise,
Your true *families,*
The ones
You most *feel* at home with,
May not be,
The ones you were born into.

* * *

I have had my share of rebelling against authority and this poem is not only about my relationship with my dad, it is also about this rebellion against God and authority, in fact anything that does not accept me as I am or deems to know me better than myself and how I should be.

I also realise I have been searching for my father's love, feeling I have never quite fulfilled his expectations of me and as I write this I can see he never quite fulfilled my expectations of him, of how he should be either.

He has however been one of my greatest teachers, thank you Dad.

Father

Fat old *fart*,
Now *hear the tear*,
Of *earth* and heart,
Of *hate* and *fear*,
Hate the rat,
Love *the heat,*
Hearth of *earth*,
A place to *eat*.
This *fate* and *era*,
That I'm *after*,
I'd *rather* be nearer,
To my *father*,
And in my *heart*,
Is where *he* lives,
I know this *art*,
For I am in his.

* * *

43

This poem shows the love I have for my mother, she was a guiding light in my life and pretty much there for me whenever I needed her. I do realise that it was not until after her death, that I started to grow up and also that I gave a lot of myself up, in order to please her. I am still incredibly grateful for all the love she showed me, thank you Mum.

Mothers

Some mothers,
Can *smother*,
For me there's no *other*,
Hero or tome,
It's where I call *home*.
Sometimes,
She talks *rot*,
But when *she's hot,*
She's hot,
From *her*,
I ask no *more*,
For even with just,
A *toe* in *the* door,
This is *the* place,
There is no *other,*
For *me* and *home*,
Is found in *mother*.

* * *

When I see medicine, I think of healing, of what is required to make us better, to cure us and the more I look at this I see that healing is wholeness and not the absence of pain. For so long I have thought of it as just that, an absence of pain and now I see, true healing is wholeness, which includes everything, especially the ability to feel whatever is present and maybe disease is just the reflection of the dis-ease we feel within ourselves.

Medicine one

Medicine – Me I see in,
And maybe the 'd' is the dance of discovery,
The door,
Just waiting to be opened,
To find the real you.

* * *

Medicine too

Me and mine,
I deem to dine,
To toss the dice,
Of men and mice,
And oh how nice,
To free my mind,
For me to end,
My need to mend.

P.S.
Am I mad?
To feel so sad,
To do you good,
It has to be bad,
or
Does it!

* * *

Following on from medicine, I came across the big 'C', cancer, the very word bringing fear into the hearts of many, hearing tales of people dying within days of hearing this prognosis, giving up on life at the very mention of the name. Well, what if cancer is a terrorist attack within our self, a voice, after being unheard for so long turns to violence and what if it is time to open our hearts to listen to our deepest fears and pain, not having to do anything with it but just a willingness to be present.

Cancer

Cancer has *an ear*,
Are you listening?
And it wants you to *care*,
Are you listening?

Can you step out of the *race*?
Are you listening?
For death has dealt *an ace*,
Are you listening?

Can you stop being *an* also *ran*?
Are you listening?
And start being all you *can*,
Are you listening?

Well *are* you?
Are you *near* to listening,
Can you *care*?
Are you listening?
Well!
Are you?
Well!

* * *

Once again I came up against what is acceptable and what is not and asked myself, who chooses? Who decides? And what if it is only when something is made unacceptable, that it actually becomes a problem! Then I saw the word 'heartbeats,' the very sign of life and within this word there is not only both **hate** and **beast** but also **breathes** – another essential sign of life. So in a nutshell what I am getting at is Life includes everything.

Heartbeats

A heart beats,
The earth breathes,
A star hears,
The rest at ease.
Earth to *star,*
And *breath* to *heart,*
The beats are set,
The rest to *start.*

And *better the heart,*
That has all *these,*
The earth, the hate,
The beast, the trees.
As beast has heart,
And hates the best.
Beat, stab and bash,
Then *tears* and *rest.*

So *bathe the beast,*
And *taste that treat,*
As this heart breathes,
To *the earth's beat.*
A breath, a stare,
A sea of *tears,*
A breast that's bare,
And *a heart that hears.*

* * *

A shield has so many uses, a defence against your enemy or protection to help you face that enemy, something to hide behind, a form of decoration and a record of your achievements. For me I saw a shield as something to hide behind, maybe even to protect others from me, I also saw that every one else has their own shield to.

Shield

She lies, she hid,
He held the *lid,*
Lie or *die*
Hill or *dell,*
Less is more,
To *hide is hell.*
This *shield is,*
A *side I see*,
Both *his* and mine,
It's not just me.

* * *

Now I know I have already written a poem called 'Believe' but when I saw **beliefs** had both **lies** and **fibs**, well what could I do, I just had to write another poem.

Beliefs

Of course *life is* an illusion,
Why else would live and *life*,
Both have *lie* in them.

And as for your *beliefs,*
Why would you trust any of these?
For here there's found both *lies* and *fibs.*

And *I* know they say, ignorance *is bliss*,
But do you really want to spend,
The rest of your *life,* feeling like this.

So what *is* the truth, that *lies* beneath,
The *self* to *see* in your *beliefs*,
To *feel, if I* be, then *life* just *is.*
Be life or *belief*
Your choice.

* * *

With relationships, I was actually looking for a word that had all the letters I wanted and as always like magic this word appeared and it is magnificent, it holds so many words within it, I have barely touched the surface of them and could have easily created many more verses. This poem is about our relationships with everything not just our partners but with ourselves as well.

Relationships

Relationships are an art, and do you play your *part*,
Or can you be *real*.
Like *a ship to the shore, let the lions roar*,
Or do *lips*, you have *to seal*.

Can you *open* up your *heart*, and *learn* from *the start*,
To relate to one another,
As every *plant has a season*, do *not* follow without *reason*,
But *let* your *heart, steer a path, to the other.*

Can you *listen* and be *still*, for *the silent* moment *till,*
Each *heart has* time *to hear.*
To shelter from *the rain, or sit* with *hate* and *pain*,
And honour, every *trial* and every *tear.*

Then atone, don't *retaliate,* and be *at one, not separate*,
For *neither's sinner, nor a saint,*
Open your *heart and listen, release the pain* and free *the passion,*
Then see potential, not restraint.

For life is no rehearsal and don't take anything personal,
And realise in this instant,
To say hello to loneliness and see all as oneness,
It's essential that you're present.

Relationships are the artist and to see what your part is
In all these many patterns,
Be still and rest at ease, be open to release,
Then happiness just happens.

* * *

I wrote '**Fixed**', after a meeting with my son and one of his friends, they were both struggling with their relationships and I just wanted to help them but soon realised I could take none of their pain away. This in turn was very painful for me as I felt so helpless and as I sat with this helplessness I was transported back to a memory of being a small child trying to make it alright for my mum, I could not do it then any more than I could do it now. This left me desperate, if only I could fix it all for them, then my life would be okay.

Fixed

Please don't *fix* me, I'm not broken
I am energy in motion
I only break when being fixed,
My heart tied up and sunk with bricks
And I *die* to these *FX*.
Each shape I need to fit
Myself I must forget,
Lost to the moment
My hands reach out in torment
To cling to something lasting
Not open now, they're grasping,
Lost to the real me
This ever flowing energy.

Please don't *fix* me, I'm not broken
I am energy in motion
And I break when being *fixed*.

To hear those dreaded words
With finger wagging pose,
'The trouble with you is',
Well, it's none of your business
What the trouble with me is,
Sort out your own life
Look at your own strife,

Don't put it on me
This pain that you feel,
It's of your own making
It's nothing I've taken,
Don't try and shame me
So you are blame free.

Please don't *fix* me, I'm not broken
I am a being in full motion
And it breaks me when you *fix* me.

Each change that I make
I feel this heart break,
Your love or disgrace
Between a rock and a hard place,
No longer true to myself.
When you loved me before
You wanted my all,
So much is now wrong
How in hell do I belong?
And it hurts to be *fixed*
To *die* in little bits,
My heart set in stone
So lost and alone.

Please don't *fix* me, I'm not broken
I'm energy in motion
And it breaks me when I'm *fixed*.

I want to stay open
And heal this heart breaking,
But how can I do this
To stay open and true with,
I need your help here, please give.
If I open my heart
Don't tear it apart,
I'm so tender and raw

I can't take any more,
I love you so much
But if I'm not enough,
There's no more I can do
To love and be true.

Please don't *fix* me, I'm not broken
I'm all these energies in motion
And they break when being *fixed*.

Of course I rebel
And make your life hell,
That's no way to live
So painful to be with,
To face ourselves and still give
These blocks of the heart
That tear us apart.
Is there another way?
To be here and to stay,
Let's find another dance
And give ourselves another chance,
Still in our own truth
With hearts open to love.

Please don't *fix*, me I'm not broken
I am being in full motion,
I see you're being to
And I won't *fix* you.

* * *

This poem is a follow on from 'Fixed' and it is about remembering who we really are and in its simplicity, gathering in all the parts of our self, just as we are.

Remember

Remember,
Remember me,
Remember be,
Re – member.

* * *

Beloved also follows on from 'Fixed' because once I stopped trying to mend the situation and started to accept life, mine as well as others, everything became simpler. I no longer felt how I used to about myself, there was this deeper acceptance within. I also realised that it is just as important to let love in, as it is, to let love out.

Beloved

Be,
Be love,
Be loved,
B E L O V E D
Be loved.
Be love,
Be.

* * *

In belonging I just saw so many ways we could belong and be long.

Belonging

Belong in this body,
Stay awhile,
Open to every precious moment,
Be long in this body.

Belong in this body,
Feel all,
From the apex to the base,
Be long in this body.

Belong in this body,
Enter fully,
Wholehearted in the present,
Belong in this body.

Belong in this body,
Feel connection,
Everything in you and you in everything,
Belong in this body.

Belonging,
The *longing* to *be*,
And the *being* that *longs*
Belonging.

* * *

Surrender is not so much about giving up, again it is about acceptance, it is about stopping the war against life, against reality, because as Byron Katie says 'Argue with reality and you will lose but only 100% of the time' and there is a relief, to just accept life as it is, without having to change anything, or put it right but free to live life fully present to what is.

Surrender

Surrender, the *sure ender*,
To *rend us under*,
I *see* no *end* here,
Unless I *surrender*.

To *ensure* my needs,
I *send* a *runner*,
There's no *end* here,
Unless I *surrender*.

To *endure* the *run*,
Seeds under the *sun*,
Still no *end* here,
Unless I *surrender*.

Undressed seen nude,
Unused and *rude*,
This war *ends* here,
When I *surrender*.

* * *

Intimacy, is about opening up, it is an invitation to let someone in, a closeness and sharing of oneself, and a willingness to meet at ever deeper levels.

Then I heard 'intimacy' was 'into-me-see', well, how fabulous is that.

Intimacy

Intimacy,
It's time to begin,
To let you *in*.

To see who *I am,*
Past *many an act,*
That keeps me *intact*.

Time to see the real me,
Into-me-see,
Intimacy.

I am in, intimacy.

* * *

Dilemmas are always about choices, which ones to make, which path to take and have you ever noticed, that when you go to bed to sleep on it, the choice is obvious in the morning. This is what this poem is about, when we try to make a decision with just our heads, there is rarely clarity, it is only when we stop and let go, that the perfect solution is found, it comes from a deeper place than just our minds, there is an internal wisdom within us all, that holds all the answers and when we stop searching, it is able to filter through to our awareness.

Dilemma

Die to the *lie.*
Dial me,
I am.

* * *

Dilemmas

All these *dilemmas*,
What should *I* do?
So many choices,
And *I* haven't *a* clue.
So
Have no *idea*,
Have no *aim*,
Just
Dial me,
I AM.

When you *see dilemmas*,
In reverse, there's *same lid,*
Each *a* distraction,
Whether *smile* or *sad.*
Just
Have no *idea*,
Have no *aim*,
Still
Dial me,
I AM.

Forgive *all dilemmas*,
The need for *ideal*,
Just *dial me, I am,*
The ready *made meal*,
Yes
Still no *idea*,
Still no *aim*,
Still
Dial me
I AM

* * *

Again just seeing the words within words and I just loved this when I saw it.

Give

Have you ever
noticed
that G I V E
is in
rec E I V in G,
well
I just have
and
I thought I would
share it with
you.

* * *

The poem 'Justice' came about when I heard 'just is' instead. This poem is once again about acceptance and is linked with the poem 'Surrender'.

Justice

It really depends, whose side you are on,
If the ref's decision *is* right or wrong,
And *justice is* seen to be done.
Just this, *just is.*

And they say all's fair in love and war,
But only winners want to keep the score,
And *justice is* less not more.
Just this*, just is.*

So where do your allegiances lay,
Is it only your side or the love of play,
And remember *just* this, *it's* only a game.
Just this, *just is.*

Let's stop the search, the need for proof,
And look to the heart, for a deeper truth,
And *just* this moment, your soul will soothe.
Just this, *just is.*
Yes let's get the *juice* out of life,
And live,
Just this, *just is.*

* * *

'Celebration' was a poem waiting to be written for so long and my inspiration came from Marion, my dear friend and mentor. It was created to celebrate the beginning of her new life, in a new home and on an amazing journey.

Thank you, Marion.

Celebration

Where there is
A P R E C I A T I O N
open into this
C R E A T I O N
diving deeply, in this great
O C E A N
and resting as
O N E.

O N E
being this
O C E A N
of
C R E A T I O N
what a wonderful
C E L E B R A T I O N.

* * *

The poem 'Grace' was initiated by Ray my beloved, when he came into the office while I was busy writing and said, 'Have you done GRACE' and then proceeded to recite a few lines, which I can no longer remember but they were enough to inspire me to write this poem.

Thank you, Ray.

Grace

Have *a care*
            Lend an *ear*
                        Stop the *race*
                        And
                                    Live in *Grace*.
So what the *rage*
            Step out the *cage*
                        Play the *ace*
                        And
                                    Live in *Grace*.
Slow the *car*
            Drop down the *gear*
                        There is no *race*
                        To
                                    Live in *Grace*.
You are the *age*
            This is your *era*
                        Be the *ace*
                        That
                                    Lives in *Grace*.
It takes great courage
            To live in *Grace*
                        To be with *rage*
                                    To stop the *race*.
So just remember
            You are
                        The *ace*
                                    In *Grace*

OH!
And look
OUR GRACE
Is
Right here in
COURAGE.

* * *

So what do you trust in? I now trust in Grace, the inner wisdom that we all can meet in our hearts. I can now let go of needing to know how my life should work for me to be okay, well most of the time, (I admit it, I can still be a control freak!). This poem was inspired by my meeting with Gangaji and realising from it that I no longer needed to sit at the feet of a guru, to seek answers from a wiser being, because now there is a wisdom within me that is as trustworthy as anything outside of me, at last I understood we have a choice, we can either go within or go without.

Trustworthy

Who you are is always *trustworthy*,
How you are, is not,
Who you are, rests in *truth*,
How you are, does not.

How you are looks for *worth*,
And prone *to worry*,
Is often *hurt* and in a *hurry*,
Questions *why*? Then tells a *story*,
Has *to try*, but still not *worthy*.
Sees the *worst* in *you*,
And not the *truth* in *you*.

So now *you* have a choice of *two*,
Do *you trust how*?
Or do *you trust Who*?
And it's not that *who* is more holy than *how*,
Because it's not,
It is just that…

Who you are is always *trustworthy*,
And *how you* are is not!

68

And it's fun *to* see, those of *us*,
Who only ever want *to* be a '*who*'
Because we think it is the right thing *to* do,
And never want to be a '*how*',
Because that's not living in the 'now',
And the joke is.
In that very moment,
We are not 'who-ing',
We are actually 'how-ing'.

* * *

I noticed that whenever I tried to name something it was to capture its essence so that I could recognise it in the future, but what if in the naming I limited the essence. I wonder can anything ever truly be named, well can it?

I am

I'm not a noun,
I am a verb,
I'm not a name,
I am more than words,
Because,
I am not a static thing,
I am for ever changing.
And,
I am not in the doing,
I am in the being,
For,
I'm not a human doing,
I am a human being.

* * *

These are some of the words that I found when looking for 'soul' within words and they speak for themselves.

Absolutely

Absolutely see the *beauty*,
Of your *soul beat*.

Be the *soul beat*,
of
Absolute,
With the *soul tide*,
of
Solitude,
In the *great tide*,
of
Gratitude.

* * *

This poem was also inspired after meeting Gangaji, and both this poem and 'Trustworthy' were created from the wisdom I received, while sitting in her presence. Thank you Gangaji.

Wound

To *undo* the *wound*,
Own now and you've *won*,
Then it's really *down* to you,
Do you trust love?
Or *do* you trust your *wound*?

* * *

So what is a parasite? Something that lives off its host giving nothing back in return, sounds a bit like the human race to me! This poem is again about acceptance, what we do not accept we try to separate from.

Parasite

I see a part,
I set apart,
I separate,
Parasite.

* * *

This poem was born from a journey process I had with my friend Nicky and is about the release of energy when you take the lid off the volcano, when it has neither roof nor floor, the energy flows freely, no longer building up into a 'Vesuvius'.

This was a major changing point in my life as before I would hold onto my anger until it became uncontrollable, this was a very frightening experience for everyone, especially me and each time after this happened I would vow never to repeat it, so tied down the hatches even more, only for a bigger explosion the next time. So what a relief to be able to recognise that anger is just an energy, a vital energy to bring about action and change.

Thank you, Nicky.

Roofless and floorless

There's no roof here,
I am roofless,
There's no floor here,
I am floorless.
Flawless in my being,
And
Ruthless in my devotion to truth

* * *

This poem has taken me forever to complete and it was only after writing 'Trustworthy' that I found the 'telltale thread', the who I am, that gave me the strength and willingness to face the how I am, to go to this place of self-hatred and be present to my own tortured soul, now knowing what was really trustworthy and what was not!

Again this is about my rage against authority, many a time I have shaken a fist in the air at God, wanting to blame something out there, something outside of my life and make it responsible for my misery. It was a very painful and devastating moment when I first felt the full impact of the self-hatred I had, this was all mine and nothing to do with anyone or anything else.

This poem has been very healing for me, not only in my relationship with myself but also with my dad, my heart is now open to him and our relationship is blossoming.

Self Hatred

Self hatred,
Broken *hearted,*
Deaf to *all I feel*
Death to *all that's real*
I'd *rather* be *dead* than face *all* this…
This *fate* worse than *death.*
For nothing is *left.*
The earth a feast I *dare* not *taste,*
This *saddest* of *heart* aches.

The threat of *all that shall* not be
Ever *hated* never *free.*
Red alert lest it be *heard*
By *the father,*
Nothing is *safe*
The father hears all,
Death to *the father*
Feared and *hated,*
Hate the father

75

Tears of *defeat*
As I burn in *hell*
To *fester* for *all*.

No *star* shines *here*
In this *heartless hell,*
Haltered and *tethered*
Tarred and *feathered*,
Nothing is *free*.
All that's dear
Dashed to *the earth*
Treads falter
Lest the real be *heard*.
The fear and *dread that* in a moment
To run *hell* for *leather* from *all* this torment.
No *heart* to *shelter* in.
This *fall* from *earth,* to *hell*
The hardest, saddest thing.

For nothing is *real,*
This *false trade*
Just *a sad* and *stale rehearsal*
A fallen *star*
In *the theatre* of *referral*,
To *steel* it *all*, for *the fear*
Nothing's *here*.
The heart theft
Shattered and *sedated*,
The self left
Defeated and *deflated*.
The lethal threat at last
Death to *the hated*.

And yet…
After all this,
Still *the tell tale thread*
Left to *see*
By *all,*

Heard by every *ear that hears*
Felt by every *heart that feels.*
Dare I *alter* this *heart felt fear*
And *free the self, that's hated here,*
To *shear the tethers*
That held, hells threats
Let death be *heard*
Hell released.

Dare I?
Dare I *share* this *hell?*
Lest it be *real*
Lest I *falter*
Lest I *feel.*
Dare I?
Dare I *feel?*

Is this how I *heal?*
To take my *heart* into *hell*
And *feel,*
To *free these halters* on *all that's real*
To face *the fear*
And *the hate,*
*That fear*ful *feast*
And *dare* to *taste…*
To *taste* it *all.*

Deaf no more too how I *feel*
Death no more to *all that's real.*
To *tread the least shared*
And *hear the heart felt,*
Rather than *fester* and *defeat*
To break the *fast*
And be complete,
To rest the war
And start with peace.

* * *

I started with a prayer so now I will finish with one. This prayer is about 'breaking the fast' and opening yourself to love, both giving and receiving. It is the completion of 'Self Hatred' and is balm for the soul, here to remind us that love can be found in the most unlikely situations, where we may never have looked before and all that is required is to be open, available and willing to receive.

This prayer was inspired by Robert Holden author of the book *Happiness Now* (which I highly recommend). Anyway while reading this amazing book, I came across this prayer, with 'spontaneously available' in it and when I saw the words 'open', 'yes', 'please' and 'love' within these words, well I just had to do my thing and make this prayer my own.

Thank you Robert Holden.

Spontaneously Available

Oh, *yes please*
Let me *be open*
And
Spontaneously available
To receive
All the *love* that *is*
And
All the *love I* am.

Thank you.

Websites

Jeanette Tuppen
www.eartheartom.com

Marion Howells
www.relaxforhealth.net

Martin Young, original artwork for the book cover and website.
www.consciousnessdesigns.com

Steve Smith, Homoeopath and photographer
www.homoeopathyschool.com
http://gallery.me.com/littlemiracle1
littlemiracle1@me.com

The Journey
www.thejourney.com

Gangaji
www.gangaji.org

The Happiness project
www.happiness.co.uk